SHOES OF MEN

POETRY WITH FUN-FILLED EXAGGERATED REALITY

ARKEYA

Made with ♥ on the Notion Press Platform
www.notionpress.com

Contents

Preface

The Series of Poetry explores the perceptions of a Man who gets into various life situations in relationships but in an exaggerated manner as to bring out the comedy of things which follows him throughout. The theme of the poem is unexplored and satirical written in a casual conversational tone.

The content was purely made for fun and I hope our readers will have a good experience. Its very much a light read. "Shoes of Men" as the title suggests is quite one dimensional as only the point of view from a man's perspective is being highlighted and highly exaggerated. It was purely due to the fact that a theme was formed while writing the series of poems and that was strictly followed without deviating much.

If our readers love this line of work we would definitely look to do a second part with " Shoes of women".

Acknowledgements

This book wouldn't have been possible if not for the support of my close friends and family.

I started writing the first poem as a joke on the first day of the year 2023. Upon sharing it with my close people, they gave such overwhelming responses that it helped me to continue writing with a poem everyday till we decided to release the series as a book.

I want to take this opportunity to thank them very much as I never imagined that a day would come where a book would be released with me being the author.

I would also like to thank the popular youtube series 'Appuppan and the boys' as their show inspired me to write chapter 13 - 'Zero information conversation'.

I would also like to take this opportunity to thank my sister. Her reaction to the first poem inspired me to make a series out of this unexplored theme.

1. Man-Tiger-Wife

A man saw a tiger
Ran for his life
Hid behind a tree
Got a call from his wife
Picked up being scared
But not of the tiger
The man is no more
Cuz he ain't Arnold Schwarzenegger!

2. Pair of Fears

A man has fears
But claims to be brave
His wife grabs him by his ears
Reaction to which will get him to his early grave
Brave man claims he can take this
As mad as it sounds
His friends totally hate this
They just want his pair to be found.

3. Sorrow Wife, Bar life

A man went to a bar
Drank his sorrows away
His wife took his car
And said, "Won't pick him *No Way*"

Man called his friend and he came in a jiffy
His wife picked up a friend; the friend's wifey
Men together drank their sorrows away
Sorrows together enjoyed the night their way

At the end, the men decided to run away
After all what is life without a getaway
But the wives came to know about their plan
And said they will join as soon as they can.

4. Happy ending or is it?

A man gets new shoes for hiking
Woman refuses to go this early waking
Man has his friends, so starts packing
Woman has her health, so starts faking
Man takes care of the woman still thinking
Woman convinces the man just blinking
Friends arrive at their home hoping
Man tells he is going out for her shopping
Woman tells the man to first finish moping
Friends tell him its time for decision making
Man decides to go and start smoking
(Disclaimer: Smoking is injurious to health)
Woman decides to use it against him poking
Man gives up, leaves his credit card, goes hiking.

5. A Musical To-Do list

A man is listening to music
Misses out what his wife was saying
Wife lashes out and makes him sick
The man has no idea where this is going

Wife complains like a to-do list from day one
He bets getting out of this cannot be achieved by no one

Man cannot recall a single thing she says
Realises to accept it all like always
Wife stops and takes a break
Man goes back to music not realising his mistake.

6. Act of caring, A sad ending

A man was cooking
Wife enters the kitchen asking
Why so much time for making
Man says "I was resting"
Wife says "As if you do everything"

Man, just pauses for a moment thinking:
" He was working
Then finished cleaning
Went grocery shopping
And now he is cooking
While she was sleeping"

Wife says for once stop thinking
And get on with cooking
Man says for once stop ordering
And consider helping

Wife says this is hurting
How could you be so condescending
And goes to her room crying
Man, quickly looks up condescending
And then looks up patronizing
In the meantime, manages to finish cooking
Laughs out knowing its meaning
Concludes it was her hunger speaking
Spends the rest of the day with her consoling

One may see this as an act of caring
But it may be nothing more than a sad sad ending.

7. Vacation a sad occasion

A man decides to take a vacation
Upon hearing, wife decides the location
And reveals the destination

Man says he does not want to go to a nearby hill station
Wife says she does not wish to go too much out of station
Man expresses that he wishes to travel around the nation
Wife says it will cause her dehydration

Man asks would he ever get to pick at least on one occasion?
Wife asks why wouldn't he care for her with some emotion?
Man says for once he would like to put his plans in motion
Wife says " How could you say that it's a tricky situation "

Man checks if she can make one exception?
Wife says she does it a lot, yet the man has more expectation
Man says all he needs is a nice break and yet faces objection
Wife says these are all pigments of his imagination

At this point the man gives up and goes with her narration
He is still in disbelief and expresses it with an exclamation

Wife points out how disrespecting that is of her decision
And cancels her (which was once his too) vacation.

8. What the Tax!

A man takes a beer
Wife says " Oh Dear "
Man says it's very light
Wife says it's not right

Man claims its finally the weekend to relax
Wife says no he still needs to do their tax
Man asks gently if he can please have this one
wife says unfortunately this can't be done

Man feels sad but thinks of an idea
Wife says you can't drink while I am asleep my dear
Man is shocked how she read his thought
Wife says I know how your mind gets caught
Man at this point says he feels violated
Wife points out its alright it's not that R Rated

Man gives up and does their taxes by himself
Wife cheers up and takes a drink for herself.

9. Feel Good Wife

A man decides to go out with friends
Wife says please go have fun
The man is surprised as she usually resents
He feels after all this time he has finally won
Wife says why don't you go on a trip with them someday
They would really want that wouldn't they
Man, pinches to see if he is sleeping
And yet the wife continues speaking
Wife says call them later here for a party
Man is shocked but feels very hearty
He tells his friends and they thought he was joking
But the truth was he was just about to be waking.

10. A wedding to remember

A man was once attending a wedding
Wife says compared to ours this is nothing
Man says give them some time they will get there someday
Wife says no amount of time would help to get to where we
are today

Man is completely speechless
Wife says why don't you say something too and gets furious
Man says Yes I totally agree
To get to where we are they will need another degree
Wife says finally you make some sense
The voice inside the man said what nonsense
But outside he smiled for self defence

Wife asks who is that woman?
Man says I didn't get you which one?
Wife says you were smiling
And I saw you looking at her rather staring
Man says I didn't were you dreaming?
Wife says you can't do this to me

Man says I really didn't do anything you see

Wife asks again who is she?

Man says still on this seriously

Wife says just shut up and apologise

Man says you were right

No one could match us level wise

Even if they tried

I apologise.

11. A Friendsinking Ship

A man once told his friends
They will keep making plans every weekend
Then he got married
His friends were a bit worried
Man was not picking calls from anyone
Soon it passed many months
Then came the day when the man was finally at their doorstep
Friends had tears and told him you owe a huge debt
Man apologises for not picking up the calls
Friends say we understand you just didn't have the balls
Man told them it's not like that she is very nice
Friends told him and we thought you were wise
Man says what matters is I am here
Friends say it took you almost half a year
Man says I gotta go soon she has made some plans
Friends say " What happened to you man "
He says it's part of growing up you might have to accept
Friends say if this is growing up then it's hard to digest
What about our every weekend pact?
Man: I know I said it but it's all in the past.

12. Shopping Wife, Missing Man

A man went missing

His wife went shopping

Hours went passing

With no one quite noticing

The man tried calling

But the wife wasn't picking

Man was stuck in office sleeping

While everyone left also locking

He called his boss and a staff came opening

Man got out and went home rushing

He knows his wife would be worrying

As that's how they are, loving and caring

But he noticed the wife was missing

She was still out shopping.

13. Zero information conversation

A Man comes from a supermarket
Wife asks did you get everything in the basket
Man says I have everything on the list
Wife says you surely would have missed one or two just sit
Man says why don't you cross check first
Wife says in a moment let me quench my thirst
Man waited anxiously and clenches his fist
Wife comes back and checks the basket
Finds out no missing item from the list
Tells the man I have something to say but can't so leave it
Not everything ends badly our reading guest
sometimes things just works out for the best.

14. Man's best friend and wife

A man was being chased by a dog
He shouldn't have gone walking in the morning fog
His wife was drinking tea writing her blog
She heard some noises much like Anirudh's BGM song
It was the man trying to fend off against the dog
Wife comes out and says don't harm animals its wrong
Man says "Bite me Dog" as it was better than letting her talk
Dog gives up and goes back understanding the man's slog
They say man's best friend for a reason while the wife gawks.

15. Man Vs Wild

A Man went on a trip with his wife
She claims to know the place well and she will be his guide
So, he did not make plans
And believed his wife will take care of things as she can

M 0-0 W

Man was happy after reaching and relaxes by the river
Wife asks him where we are going for dinner
Man says I thought you would have something in mind
Wife says yes, I have my hunger and I am still being kind
Man says I recall you telling me that you will plan things
Wife says why do I have to do everything

M 0-1 W

Man takes the phone to look for places nearby
Wife says he should have taken some effort at least try
Man looks up the sky
Wife asks "What? do you deny?"
Man, still looks up and says why God why?
Wife says be quick in reply
Man says I found a Chinese place close by
Wife says no I need Thai

M 0-2 W

Man asks what's the difference?
Wife says that's racism and an offense
Man says it's just similar food don't you think
Wife says yeah now say Northeast is Chinese too and wink

M 0-3 W

Man feels very much sad
Woman is getting quite mad
She asks, "Where is my food"?
Man says enough with the drama this ain't Bollywood

M 1-3 W

Wife says how can you be this mean

Is this how you treat your woman
Man says stop creating a scene
And who are we kidding your drama is common

M 2-3 W

Wife throws a glass of water on him and says let that sink
Drama is common don't you think
Man takes off his shirt and says goodbye forever
Leaving her there in shock as he goes and dives in the river.

?

Game Based On Man-tiger-wife

Our very first poem title is also a three way game much like rock-paper-scissors.

Man-Tiger-Wife or Three way deadlock

Instructions

1. It needs 3 players. and 3 hand signs for Man, tiger and wife

2. Tiger eats the man so tiger gets the point.

3. Wife drives him crazy. She always gets the point.

4. If Wife and tiger comes face to face

the man gets to live and thus gets the point.

5. 3 players must use all 3 hand signs at least 3 times during

the match.

6. Match concludes once a player gets to 10 points.